Denise KENYON-ROUVINEZ, PH.D.
THIERRY LOMBARD
MATTHIEU RICARD
John L. WARD, PH.D.

GABS.

Why Me?

WEALTH: CREATING, RECEIVING AND PASSING IT ON

Division of The Family Business Consulting Group, Inc.

1220-B Kennestone Circle
Marietta, Georgia 30066
Tel: 1-800-551-0633
Web Site: www.efamilybusiness.com

Also in the series:

Who, Me?

FAMILY BUSINESS SUCCESSION
A PRACTICAL GUIDE FOR THE NEXT GENERATION

© Family Enterprise Publishers 2007
ISBN: 1-891652-20-6

To the many families throughout the world who have taught us that happiness and wealth can be a beautiful combination.

Detailed Table of Contents

Introduction	11
I. Why?	15
II. The Meaning of Wealth	23
Why Me?	24
What is Money?	26
New Money or Old Money?	28
Will It Last?	30
What Do *Others* Think?	32
What Do *We* Think?	34
Wealth: More Than Money	36
It's Up to Me	38
Defining Wealth	40
III. Creating Wealth	43
The Entrepreneur's Story	44
From Me to Us	46
The Next Generation Perspective	48
A Larger Family	50
Consequences of a Larger Family	52
Can Nepotism Work?	54
Growing it Again	56

IV. Parenting with Wealth — 59
- Parenting as Craft — 60
- Fundamental Truths — 62
- Special Issues — 64
- Some Tips — 66
- Parenting Paradoxes — 68

V. Managing Wealth — 71
- Know your Wealth — 74
- Define Objectives — 76
- Organize Communication — 78
- Define Family Roles and Responsibilities — 80
- Choose the Right Advisors — 82

VI. Inheriting Wealth — 85
- Identity and Self-Worth — 86
- The Meaning and Purpose of Money — 88
- Responsibility and Stewardship — 90
- Taking Charge — 92

VII. Living with Wealth — 95
- How Others See You — 96
- Uncomfortable Situations — 98
- Personal Support — 100
- Family Meetings — 102

VIII. Transmitting Wealth 105
    The Technical Side of Transmissions 106
    Distribution: Equity and Fairness 108
    Passing on Legacy Assets 110
    Letters of Wishes, Donor's Intent, Ethical Wills 112
    Communication 114

Conclusion 117
Additional Reading 121
The Authors 122
Index 124

Introduction

Wealth for the future

Is it possible to speak openly about wealth? That is the challenge that this book modestly attempts to meet, using all the accoutrements—knowledge, wisdom and even humor—that such a topic requires.

Wealth has always been a rather taboo subject, although the most ostentatious kind of wealth, the kind that doesn't fear scandal or publicity, is usually best circumventing such constraints. This is the wealth that we see splashed all over magazines, providing the tabloid press with its core product, and seemingly created for the sole purpose of inciting as much gossip and envy as possible.

Wealth that goes beyond—or beneath—appearances is a more delicate subject. Whatever the considerable privilege represented by wealth, there are different ways of being rich. This is not a matter of differentiating between those who prefer a yacht and those who prefer a mansion, nor between "external" and "internal" wealth. No, the difference we are referring to involves the meaning one gives to one's wealth and the kinds of ambition one attaches to it.

Introduction

This is as true for material wealth as for genetic wealth, for "talents" in the biblical sense and for talents in the artistic sense: between letting wealth lie fallow and cultivating it intensively. There are many possible degrees of "realization" that give wealth its myriad of different forms. The overly generic category of "the rich" contains a further division: for wealthy people, as for talented people the ultimate difference lies between those who are ambitious and everyone else; between those who want to make the best of what they have and those who are just carried along by who they are. Taken in this particular sense, ambition radically changes the meaning and the purpose of wealth. It is the factor that turns privileges into responsibilities, visions into plans, ideals into objectives, noble causes into action, dreams into reality—and money into a future.

To meet the challenge of approaching this taboo subject, we asked the French cartoonist Gabs to portray this separate world of wealth via his cartoons, which can often strike the heart of a matter more than words can. But we also needed another factor besides humor to give us some perspective—wisdom. Matthieu Ricard, Buddhist monk, interpreter for the Dalaï-Lama, renowned photographer and writer, provides this with his singular and characteristic depth. Finally, the academic knowledge

INTRODUCTION

brought by eminent family enterprise consultants Dr. Denise Kenyon-Rouvinez and Dr. John L. Ward addresses any remaining taboos not dealt with by humor and wisdom—providing important questions as well as clear guidance.

As for us, we are pleased to be associated with this volume, because its subject is especially close to our hearts. Inevitably, money is at once the raw material, the means, and the result of our profession. We have respected it as such for over two centuries, as the carpenter respects wood and the sculptor respects stone. But we respect the fortunes entrusted to us for what they are, we value them for the promise they hold. It is our greatest wish and our highest ambition that today's wealth—whether long-held or recently acquired—be *wealth for the future*, not just an end for today. Wealth is a means of building tomorrow's world.

Thierry Lombard

I

Why?

Why?

Wealth, like any tool, can be used to build or to destroy. It can facilitate well being and generosity or it can create greed and dissatisfaction, all obstacles to authentic happiness. Wealth can be a remarkable means for doing good and, consequently, can lead to a life of happiness. Wealth also carries risks. It can make one's life miserable and can lead to harming others.

How we deal with wealth, or anything, depends on our motivation and on how we experience the world. It is very difficult to predict exactly what the consequences of our decisions and actions will be, but we can always examine our state of mind. Are we motivated chiefly by selfishness devoid of compassion or by altruism and a true desire to be of benefit? Our state of mind, benevolent or malicious, is at the core of ethics.

Our motivations color our decisions and actions, just as a crystal reflects the color of the cloth upon which it rests. As the Dalaï Lama says, before we do any action we need to ask ourselves: "Are we being broad-minded or narrow-minded? Have we taken into account the overall situation or are we considering only specifics? Is our view short-term or long-term? We need to think, think, think."[1]

Our own well-being is also affected by our sense of ethics. Making others suffer ultimately will bring suffering to ourselves. On the other hand, creating happiness for others is the best guarantee of our own. Thus, ethics can be seen as a science of happiness and suffering.

Aristotle said that happiness is the goal of goals. Wealth, pleasure, rank and power are all sought for the sake of happiness. But in our striving we can forget our goal and focus on the means for their own sake. We miss the point and remain deeply unsatisfied. This is one of the traps that keep us from the pursuit of a meaningful life.

Sociological studies have shown that as Western societies become richer, their people do not become happier. As Richard Layard, professor at the London School of Economics writes: "All the evidence says that on average people are no happier today than people fifty years ago. Yet at the same time average incomes have more than doubled. We have more food, clothes and cars, bigger houses, more central heating, a shorter workweek, better work conditions and, above all, better health. Yet we are not happy."[2]

Why?

Obviously for those who lack the basic means of subsistence and for whom money is a question of survival, increased wealth makes a great difference and brings a legitimate sense of satisfaction. Beyond that, however, it has been proven that doubling or tripling our income does not further increase our true level of satisfaction.

As influential as external conditions may be, happiness, like suffering, is essentially an interior state. This understanding is the key prerequisite to living a fulfilled life. We need to discover which mental conditions sap our *joie de vivre*, and which nourish it. True happiness depends on inner conditions. Happiness is not given to us, nor is misery imposed.

The essential inner conditions for authentic happiness are loving-kindness and compassion, deep sensitivity to others' suffering and an irrepressible desire to remedy them. A person at peace with himself will contribute spontaneously to establishing peace within his family, his neighborhood, and, circumstances permitting, society at large. For wealth to make a long-term improvement in the profoundest aspects of our lives, it must therefore be imbued with positive human qualities, such as altruism and wisdom.

Matthieu Ricard

---

1. Dalai Lama *Ancient Wisdom, Modern World*, op. cit.
2. Layard, R., *Happiness, Lessons From a New Science*, London, Allen Lane, Penguin Books, 2005.

II
The Meaning of Wealth

"Seeking happiness in possessions alone is like fishing in a dry river bed."

Why Me?

Why am I so fortunate?

Why am I feeling so ambivalent about privilege?

Why am I not seen for whom I really am?

Why am I so burdened with expectations and responsibilities?

Why am I overwhelmed by the choices and challenges of managing money?

Why am I not able to talk about all this?

I am not my money. I don't want wealth to be my identity. I don't want money to dominate my life. I don't want it to damage my family and friendships.

What is Money?

The essence of these common questions and feelings is the meaning we attribute to money. What we mean by money, and by wealth, also substantially affects how we manage our money, transmit it to future generations, and live with it – the subjects of this book. Economists tell us that money is a "medium of exchange" – like beads or metal pieces. Money is also a "storehouse of value." Wealth is a large storehouse. As such, money—even wealth—is a neutral concept. Money, per se, has no emotions or feelings. It is a descriptive fact, like height or pulse rate.

People of wealth work hard to see money as neutral. They seek to not let money define them. Families with money also realize that wealth is more than money. It is not only a storehouse of value, but a storehouse of *values*. Money, of course, is also a social symbol. Unavoidably it carries many other meanings. Families of wealth talk among themselves about these symbols and how they affect their everyday life and how they want them to affect future generations. We hope this book helps your family in its discussions about money.

New Money or Old Money?

As a social symbol the meaning of money is fundamentally influenced by others and by our culture. It also changes through the generations. Business builders and wealth creators typically see wealth as a scorecard. How much money one has is a worldly measure of success gained from their ideas, skills, risk taking and unrelenting hard work. In fact, it also measures the amount of "good" provided to society. Successful entrepreneurs are usually highly valued. Governments try to encourage more of them.

Even "new money" spent extravagantly often gets the benefit of the doubt: it was earned.

Nonetheless, builders and creators are conflicted. They have fears about what the money will do to their families. They worry about physical security. More poignantly, they see their wealth as a threat to their family's emotional health. They fear that their success will snuff out the very entrepreneurial values they cherish for themselves. Will the risk taking and work ethic of future generations be suffocated, they ask.

Will It Last?

Parents who achieve and those who follow are all troubled by the old adage: "Shirt sleeves to shirt sleeves in three generations."

But, it can be a self-fulfilling prophecy. To protect against family destruction, high controlling entrepreneurs often lock up their wealth such that their children will never see or touch it. They don't appreciate that such lack of trust in family can be more threatening than the spoils of money.

Inheritors are challenged by the responsibilities of wealth. Successors commonly worry non-stop about preserving the resources and reputation of the family. They worry—even to a risk taking aversion—that things will go awry on their watch. They are trapped by being "rich on paper but poor in cash" – yet feel expected to live up to the charitable expectations fueled by previous generations. Later generations struggle with the reality that families often grow faster than their wealth. Should they personally sacrifice and devote their lives to rebuilding the wealth for more distant relatives?

"So what do you do?"

"Nothing... I'm too afraid of losing my money"

GABS.

What Do *Others* Think?

While society typically praises entrepreneurs as achievers and heroes, inheritors often are seen as lucky, unworthy, or spoiled. Imagine all those around you: in-laws, friends, employees, professional advisors, etc.—their attitudes about wealth become a part of your everyday life.

Our own attitudes about money and wealth are influenced by the society in which we live. Capitalistic societies reward material success. Mature social democracies look askance at inequalities – suspecting them to be unjust. Emerging economies see wealth as power. These different views get translated into tax policy.

Opinions on wealth are rarely so simple. In fact, friends and society send mixed messages. If money could talk, what words would it use? Evil, dirty, burden, responsibility? Reward, beauty, privilege, opportunity?

Money has ambivalent meanings. Wealth creates ambivalent feelings.

What Do *We* Think?

Money itself has no emotions, no feelings. While understanding the social context of wealth is useful, one's own meaning is what matters. We cannot control the world around us, or others' assumptions. But we can control our own beliefs and behaviors.

Some wealth creators see their material success as a way to buy social acceptability. Such beauty, of course, is only skin deep. Other successful creators see wealth as resource to be used effectively and efficiently.

Some inheritors and spouses see their gifts as repayment for the sacrifices of a youth without an involved parent or an attentive mate.

A critical distinguishing belief about money is whether it is seen as "my" money or "the" money. Possessiveness for money can lead to wealth defining the person. Thinking of money as an inanimate fact helps keep money neutral.

Wealth: More Than Money

A second distinguishing belief about money is whether money is viewed as only one form of wealth. Individuals and families have many other kinds of richness – some much more precious than money. These include spiritual wealth, happiness and health, networks of trusted relationships, knowledge and learning, a loving family, reputation, and heritage. Many families talk about enhancing and preserving these forms of wealth at least as often as how to grow and protect their financial capital.

"IF HIS SPIRIT IS AS WEALTHY AS HIS WALLET, HE SHOULD BE SAINTED IMMEDIATELY"

GABS.

It's Up to Me

Money is neutral. It doesn't have to define us. As money is a storehouse of value, wealth is a storehouse of *values*. How we spend the luxury of our time and our treasure expresses those values for generations to come. Wealth is more than money. Successful families have many other forms of capital, each deserving all our preservation and perpetuation skills.

Non-judgmental discussion of the meaning of money in family meetings is a wonderful starting point. Each family member can reflect on money's meaning in society, among their relationships, for themselves. Some families actually forge a definition or goal about wealth as part of their family constitution, or as part of their letter of wishes to future generations. Some examples follow.

Defining Wealth

"Wealth is a generous family gift of empowerment to pursue freely one's individual talents, a venturesome love of work, and a balanced life."

"Our resolve is to offer the next generation the support and education to make wealth neutral and to prepare them for the changing circumstances of their times."

"To preserve family wealth as best as possible without inhibiting individual freedom nor sacrificing our relationships with one another as a family."

"We see our wealth as a platform to do good."

III

Creating Wealth

"It is fine to travel along your path with speed and determination. But remember that the happiness or suffering that lies at the end of your journey depends on the direction you have chosen for your life."

The irony of creating significant wealth is that doing so often brings vulnerabilities for its own preservation and healthy transmission.

The Entrepreneur's Story

Many an entrepreneur has lamented, "It's not my fault! I am just doing what I love to do…and am at the right place at the right time. The more I work the more wealth problems I'm creating, but I can't stop myself. It's my life." How can something so naturally beautiful as substantial achievement and generating jobs and joy for others have another side?

Whether entrepreneurs or wealth creators are made or born, they are rare. They have certain geniuses, and they almost always admit to some luck.

Let's start at the beginning. Usually, young in life, entrepreneurs are frustrated in fighting for their beliefs. They resolve to go it alone and choose a lofty dream. They work long hours. They overcome incredible obstacles. They depend on others – sometimes finding great disappointment. They experiment; they constantly challenge how things are.

Perhaps they risked it all. Sometimes ethical shortcuts are taken. Survival is at stake.

From Me to Us

The entrepreneur grows in age and success. The entrepreneur's family grows older and larger.

Entrepreneurs often learn some challenging habits with future consequences:

– Hard work on the job was essential and helped defend absence to a sacrificing family.
– Sharing work's trials and tribulations at home was relieving and redeeming.
– Secrecy and privacy avoided unwanted problems.
– Self-reliance worked better than trusting others.
– Faithfulness was for those who had been loyal.
– Money solved all sorts of issues – at work and at home.
– Saving was the best insurance against inevitable surprises.
– Sharing the earnings became a way to reconnect with the community and make good on debts they felt due.
– Things could always be improved – including children's efforts and discipline. Perfection was an unrelenting goal.

The values of work, sacrifice, frugality, independence and conservatism became core family values. They will shape the family's method of transmitting, preserving and growing their wealth.

The Next Generation Perspective

The next generation hears more about the problems of work and less about its joys. The next generation feels it has sacrificed, too – sacrificed parental time. Gifts and money are often substituted for time and involvement. The next generation is told that all the effort and sacrifice is for their benefit. Instead, they suspect that a balanced life is more valuable than money. They have grown accustomed to their parents' lifestyles. They don't remember as well the early days of struggle, making ends meet while trying to find success.

Money isn't perceived as a scarce resource anymore. They spent their teenage years in a nice neighborhood, going to good schools and enjoying affluent vacations.

Eventually the next generation becomes guardians of the family's assets. They are not sure the work is really fulfilling. They know it is nearly impossible to meet their parent's expectations or follow in their footsteps and recreate the magnificent miracle of the founding generation.

A Larger Family

In-laws arrive and live in the shadow of a powerful controlling personality. Often successors have the additional challenging requirement to forge a partnership with their siblings. Both they and their spouses long for private, independent time. Their children, the cousin generation are born.

The entrepreneurial couple loves all their children and treats them the same financially even though they can't all be equal in running a business or supervising financial assets. The sibling partnership requires a lot of tolerance and generosity to succeed. That's expensive.

The entrepreneurial couple also loves each of their grandchildren equally—and wants the best education and life for them.

The entrepreneur's estate planning starts late and is driven by advisors who want to justify their contribution by saving taxes. In the entrepreneur's circle of business friends there are too many examples of new generations letting leisure evaporate work and money not guarded carefully.

Consequences of a Larger Family

These circumstances lead to several predictable, troubling results:

– There has been little communication at home about business, money and life.
– Inheritance plans are set to save taxes and protect the next generation from easy access to money.
– Equality among siblings makes decision making more complex.
– Next generation leaders are fearful of risking their family's capital and reputation. Preservation trumps entrepreneurship.
– Equality among cousins is an illusion.
– Cousins have less exposure and affinity to the business.

The second generation might respond to their challenges by leading lives opposite of their parents. The third and later generations don't know firsthand the requirements of financial success. "Shirt sleeves to shirt sleeves…" seems inevitable.

Can Nepotism Work?

Despite the above classic scenario, nepotism in family wealth creation can and does work. We have seen scores of examples; much of these are a result of parenting practices discussed later. In addition, consider the following advantages of the second generation:

- They have seen success.
- They know what it takes.
- They learned the importance of relationships.
- They have a perspective of time and risk.
- They know people who can help.
- They have a heritage of special capabilities.

All these advantages can also be taught to the cousins, if grandparents are willing and if parents have emotional peace with their past.

Successful family successors have learned they must define their own wealth creation strategy. They built on past success but added their own passion and vision. They adapted to the changing times while preserving the core values of success.

Growing it Again

New generations may begin to diversify the family's holdings. Some of those extensions are platforms for ventures.

Counter-intuitively, assuring low risk security for each family member allows the wealth creators to seek higher goals. And the more freedom offered the members of the family, the stronger will be the commitment of all to the challenge of renewed wealth creation.

But wealth creation and re-creation can't be everyone's skill or interest. Happily, families have siblings or cousins to draw on. For those in the next generation bravely following in the footsteps of the entrepreneur, nothing is more valuable than the emotional support and informed consent of others in the family.

IV

Parenting With Wealth

"To be a good parent is to be a living example of caring and altruism. The messenger must be the message."

Parenting as Craft

Parenting is the most personal of life's tasks. Prescriptions are resisted and restricting – for good reasons. Each parent wants to learn the craft his or her own way, using experiences from childhood and family history, while collaborating with their partner. For those parents not reared with wealth, their experience is limited and their worries heightened. A powerful metaphor conveys the craft of parenting well…Parenting is not like molding a sculpture from clay, it is more like gardening – preparing the plot, nurturing the plant, keeping out the weeds, worrying about the unpredictable weather.

The clay sculpture, however beautiful, becomes rigid and brittle. The garden yields continuous joy and new surprises. The work of the gardener never ends, even as the garden matures. The beauty of the garden is in the eye of the beholder. Similarly, parenting children of wealth is driven by the parents' own definition of money. If wealth is believed neutral, parents can rely on some fundamental truths. If wealth is an obsession, the fears become paralyzing and self-fulfilling.

Fundamental Truths

Putting wealth aside, the basics become clearer:

— Values are learned at home.
— Generosity is natural, particularly if reinforced.
— Children do as they see, more than as they are told.
— Clarity and consistency set the way.
— Choices with consequences teach confidence.
— Each child is different.
— Not all have equal competences; each deserves dignity.
— Parenting is never perfect; children forgive; mistakes are okay.

These truths are all the more significant in families of wealth. The values taught trump the materialism of money. Charity and philanthropy give money a purpose. The lifestyle example of parents significantly sets future expectations and needs. The example of parents also shapes whether money defines the individual or the individual defines wealth in all its forms. Too many choices without consequences are the inheritor's greatest challenge. Parents cannot control the future forever.

As many have said, the fundamental lesson for parents with wealth is: It's not what you have, but what you do with what you have.

Special Issues

Parents with substantial financial means face many particular questions.

- Where and how do we live? Many live near others of similar station to share the spotlight. Others choose to take a step back to demonstrate modesty.
- What and when do we tell our kids about their circumstances and future? Secrecy breeds distrust and low self-esteem. Too much information too soon detours a normal life.
- Do we treat all the kids equally in information and gifts? Surely there are situational exceptions and, surely, there is a sense of fairness in equal treatment.
- What do we mean by work? Some believe earning money is the ultimate security and equips one with a work ethic. Some feel the drive for achievement with disciplined effort defines work, even if there is no pay.
- How much do we pool the children's interests in shared activities, or how much do we facilitate free choice and independence? Regardless, teaching the skills of conflict management and joint decision-making makes whatever holds the family together stronger.

Some Tips

Though each situation is different and all parents have their own philosophies, some lessons from others are widely held.

— Personal stories and personal letters carry special weight through the generations.
— Teach financial literacy young, at the dinner table.
— Allowances are dividends; family chores are expected.
— Allowances are one part spending, one part saving, one part charity.
— Some anonymous family giving deepens the meaning of philanthropy.
— Never say "we can't afford it" (unless it's true). Instead, emphasize priorities and wise choices.
— Urge independent, self-reliant experiences before economic independence is gifted.
— The gift of money offers the next generation the opportunity to do what they want to do. Too much, too soon tempts them to do nothing.
— During family meetings, emphasize the other forms of capital – education, reputation, social networks and heritage.

Parenting Paradoxes

In the end, parenting in privileged families requires good judgment at balancing predictable paradoxes.

- Trust others, cautiously. There are times others will take advantage. But being able to trust is essential.
- Be secure, without being paranoid. Physical security is extremely important. Education and personal responsibility are empowering.
- Don't wear your money, nor hide it. Excess in either direction takes away your authentic identity.
- Wealth is a privilege and a responsibility. Seeing stewardship as an opportunity reconciles this tension.
- Cherish individual freedom and promote family as a close community. Without one, the other is compromised.
- Treat each family member as special and all family members equally.

Families discuss these paradoxes. Parents share their philosophy through family letters.

The fundamental parenting paradox is to give each child both roots and wings. Roots provide the security to risk and explore. Wings bring rewards back to all the family.

V
Managing Wealth

"Accumulating wealth for its own sake, is like collecting ink, paper and pens without ever actually writing the book of your life."

"Look at stocks as businesses, look for businesses you understand, run by people you trust and…leave them alone for a long time."
Andrew Kilpatrick of "Permanent Value"

It is difficult to understand and master the complexities of the investment world, offering as it does a wide variety of opportunities: stocks, bonds, hedge funds, investment funds (mutual, "green", "ethical", specialized), currencies, art, real estate, private equity, commodities, etc.

Kilpatrick's sentence suggests that managing wealth goes beyond cold numbers; it is work, life, and must be understood "organically."

Negotiating this maze of possibilities is particularly difficult for young heirs receiving their first shares and dividends and for spouses who have never been involved in the management of the family wealth. It is often not easy for the wealth creators themselves.

Well-managed wealth can become stable and grow, but wealth disappears much more easily than it is created. Five principles will help. 1: Know your wealth; 2: Define objectives; 3: Organize communication; 4: Define family roles and responsibilities; 5: Choose the right advisors.

1. Know Your Wealth

Managing wealth involves a serious knowledge of it. Wealthy people, whether they are entrepreneurs or inheritors, should know what they have, what they earn and what their investments earn.

Evaluating one's portfolio should be carried out regularly. This is equally true whether the wealth is invested in businesses, equities, real estate or other investments. Not keeping a close eye on performance – even when professionals are in charge means uncontrolled risk and a higher chance of misfortune. Performance can be measured in many ways. Tools used can be simple or sophisticated, but they need to measure some fundamental factors: a) What is the gross return vs. the goals set? b) How is each investment performing relative to its sector? c) Are total costs under control, including the cost of administration?

Benchmarking goals and results within their respective sectors and exchanging and comparing with people in similar situations will assure that the strategies set are right; that performance is "correct;" and that assets are appropriately allocated. This is necessary control, but control is useless without a clear idea of personal objectives and constraints.

2. Define Objectives

Individuals and families alike need to decide whether they want to invest for the short term or the long term (one or more generations), and the level of risk they are ready to assume. In other words they have to decide whether to prioritize slow but steady long-term growth or high-risk/high-return investments – or what combination of these approaches they wish to adopt.

Individuals and families need then to assess their overall financial needs. What is their lifestyle? Do they want to work at all? Do they want to live well, have an affluent retirement? Do they expect the family wealth to provide for it all or are family members expected to be self-sufficient? Answers to these questions will decide the returns and risks needed to cover their needs and the cost of investment, and the additional return needed to preserve or to grow their wealth.

Then, based on these assessments and their values, they define an investment philosophy—where to invest, where not to invest, levels of reinvestment, tolerated levels of risk, performance goals, etc.—and they identify exit strategies to limit potential losses.

3. Organize Communication

No matter how deep his or her expertise, no one will manage wealth optimally if they do not know and understand peoples' wishes. Everyone must communicate clearly what their investment philosophy is and what their objectives are. Family members also need to make sure that the guidelines they set in terms of diversification, areas in which to invest, risk and performance are respected.

This is not an easy task. It requires significant training and education to reach a sufficient level of understanding – not to become an expert, but to be able to understand what issues are at stake, which decisions need to be made and whether or not the wealth is managed wisely and effectively.

Making decisions when faced with a multitude of specialists each with their own, often unintelligible jargon can be quite daunting. Don't be afraid to ask questions if something is not understood and have the courage to ask for explanations until both parties understand each other.

4. Define Family Roles and Responsibilities

Whether they are the money creators or the inheritors, wealthy families will inevitably come to a point where they will have to decide whether their wealth is invested collectively or split and invested individually. There is no right or wrong, but each choice has consequences.

Splitting the inheritance can avoid conflicts and allows each individual to lead his or her life as he or she wishes. However, there are two disadvantages: each investor has a much-reduced scope for investment and diversification; and individuals are more likely to make hasty decisions without the wisdom born from group decisions.

Keeping the wealth together and investing it collectively produces synergy. Learning together can be fun. But as the number of people involved grows, there is more potential for different goals and conflict. It might be a good idea to structure the collective wealth so that it can be divided easily among the individuals at a later date, should the need arise.

Managing and governing the family thus becomes just as important as managing its wealth.

5. Choose the Right Advisors

"Somebody once said that in looking for people to hire, you look for three qualities: integrity, intelligence, and energy. And if they don't have the first, the other two will kill you."

Omaha World Herald, February 1, 1994

Managing wealth is seldom a full-time activity, thus the entourage of financial, legal and tax advisors should be carefully selected.

It is important to identify who will work well, with one's best interests at heart – or, who to turn to when a problem arises. The choice is based on the competence and trustworthiness of those advisors. While competence is relatively easy to assess, trust takes time to build.

Knowing whom to trust, and being willing to listen to and respect their advice, are crucial. Young inheritors and spouses not previously involved are urged to identify two or three very trustworthy people from among friends, family and advisors to assist them.

Ultimately, managing wealth is managing relationships and information.

VI

Inheriting Wealth

"External wealth is an ever changing mosaic of lights and shadows. It is the steady glow of internal wealth that will enlighten your life."

Identity and Self-Worth

While those who create wealth are often at ease with affluence, inheritance has been known to sometimes lead its beneficiaries into depression and other psychological or dependence issues. Though such extremes are relatively rare, it is true that most inheritors are ill at ease with wealth, at least in their younger years.

Why is this? A closer look at the differences between wealth creators and inheritors gives some important clues. Wealth creators have a tremendous "sense of self"—they have built their own success. Their wealth is a result of their own hard work, luck and flair.

Inheritors are born into affluence and of successful parents, maybe a line of several successful generations. What a daunting perspective: what is left for them to accomplish? What if they were to distinguish themselves by failing? Such thoughts can be paralyzing. But those who are determined to make their own mark in their own way will find their own identity and self worth.

The Meaning and Purpose of Money

Certain questions have a fundamental impact on the lives and behavior of inheritors: What is my motivation when everything is available? What is there to do when so much has been achieved already? Is making more money going to make any difference when so much money is already there? When is the time to start "doing something serious" when all the time in the world seems available?

Yet, drive, pride and motivation are important factors contributing to a balanced life and are essential for preserving and growing the family wealth. Many inheritors find new motivation when they stop focusing on what they have and start dreaming about what to do with it.

Identifying a new goal, and using one's wealth as a springboard from which to achieve it, represents an opportunity for inheritors to prove themselves. The wealth they received may feel like an "unearned" privilege, but treasuring and using it as an enabler to do something creative, something useful for themselves or their families, something meaningful for their community or for society at large can be the foundation on which to build their own contribution to the world.

Responsibility and Stewardship

An in-depth analysis of dynasties that have successfully transmitted their businesses or wealth through several generations reveals that at some stage, possibly in one of the relatively early generations, inheritors stop being "masters" and become "servants." They begin to develop a sense of stewardship towards the family wealth. They feel a sense of responsibility to take care of their family, to nurture the family assets and to transmit them to the next generation. They are the custodians of the family wealth and they want to ensure that it endures.

They become responsible not only for themselves but also for their whole family and for future generations. It can be felt as a burden but also as a privilege – the opportunity to contribute to the family's continuing success.

These "stewards" often have a real heart-felt desire and ambition to perpetuate not only the family's wealth, but also its motivation, philosophies and values. They see themselves as part of a chain of continuous development and view the family adventure as exciting and enriching.

Taking Charge

To lead a fulfilling life, inheritors need the wisdom to accept their circumstances. Inheritance can create envy around them and ambivalent feelings within them. These feelings have to be acknowledged as much as the fears that affluence can generate – but inner peace and genuine happiness will only come with a true and profound acceptance of their situation and a sense of purpose to achieve something with their wealth.

There is nothing more important for inheritors than to have the confidence to be the people they are. To be successful, they need to make the most of their life on their own terms, by their own definition, following their own innermost aspirations while perpetuating the family legacy. It is up to their parents to let them blossom and mature, and to be proud of them.

Being oneself does not mean simply accepting all one's faults as inevitable, or quitting as soon as things get a little tough. To be at ease with themselves, inheritors need to find their own space, to discover their own potential and to fulfill it. They need to embrace the opportunity given to them and turn it into a positive experience.

VII

Living With Wealth

"Wealth and possessions can only create our image. They are never a reflection of who we really are."

How Others See You

Personal or family wealth brings awkward moments. Children ask, "How rich are we?" Friends can't afford the same luxuries. Relations need a business loan. Employees have a personal problem. Charities think you can afford more than you have. In-laws can't be as generous to their grandchildren as you. Advisors become dependent. Do prospective friends like my money or me? In some cultures the general public believes privilege is unjust.

Counter intuitively; the outcome of these moments is fully in our own hands. Others are more uncomfortable. They feel insecure, perhaps envious. They presume for themselves less power, lower status. The more they have these feelings the more aggressive they seem.

Interaction with others is an exchange of self-concepts. If the less privileged person feels inferior and the privileged person feels self-guilt or unworthiness, the outcome is rarely good. Bad decisions are made or bad feelings result. Ironically, the more the privileged person is comfortable with himself or herself, the better things work.

Uncomfortable Situations

Growing accustomed to personal wealth and privilege in social situations typically follows a developmental cycle. The first stage is denial. "No, I'm not part of that family." "I doubt I'll ever see the family's money." Deceiving is, of course, uncomfortable and sends an unfortunate message to the next generation. In the extreme, people give away all their money or live a life not using or enjoying their means. The second stage is to counterattack the person who brings the discomfort. Sometimes a cut off reply like, "I don't feel that's an appropriate request" is useful. But if the relationship is valued, such a strategy isn't helpful. Then those of privilege often just absorb the discomfort. They remember their parents' or counselors' admonition: "Have a thick skin." "Those others can't help it."

In time, families of wealth are comfortable with themselves and simply offer, "Yes, we have been very fortunate."

They may have the security and skill to empathetically support the person of less means. "I can understand how you think I can provide your need for investment capital. You are important to me. Can I help by brainstorming other avenues for finding what you need?"

Personal Support

With wealth come many blessings, but also—surprising to many—a lot of work and time. Pursuing a vocation and raising a family makes for a very full life.

Personal wealth brings the responsibilities of financial education and family governance roles to oversee advisors and enterprises. Society expects more of those who have more. Active engagement in civic and charitable affairs is positive – giving back while extending the family's social and reputation capital. Some in the family also have the passion to recreate the family's wealth.

Without help, one can become overwhelmed. Families learn that staff and office support are necessary – to assure time for parenting; to do what's done excellently; to help others. A Family Office becomes a great support and great resource.

Another great support and resource is the Family Foundation. In part, the foundation can politely deflect unwelcome requests and help with administrative tasks. More importantly, the family foundation becomes a source of energy for the family.

Family Meetings

The greatest support for families of wealth is a supportive family. As the generations pass, that isn't automatic.

Farsighted families organize themselves to address their shared needs and exciting prospects. Regular meetings of the entire family evolve into a family council leading the planning and, perhaps, even family council committees sharing the leadership for family fun, family communications, family history and family education.

Education on parenting, philanthropy, and financial literacy give the family skills and confidence. Sharing experiences with the benefit of family intimacy and trust brings great comfort and commitment.

Many families grow their own competence on the meaning of money and how to extend the other forms of wealth. They explore together and define for future generations the challenges of privilege, the skills needed to deal with the circumstances of money, goals to grow and preserve and share wealth, a philosophy for the legitimacy of private wealth and strategies to enhance their heritage.

As Mark Twain famously said, "You never really know someone until you share an inheritance with them." And that can be really good!

VIII

Transmitting Wealth

"He who is deeply content at heart holds a treasure in the palm of his hand."

The Technical Side of Transmissions

So many elements come into the transmission of wealth. Some are obvious, some less so, but all are important to ensure a clean and effective transmission. Technical elements often come first to mind. They are easier to deal with and have a relatively low emotional impact as external experts are available to provide solutions – lawyers and notaries for wills; estate and tax planners; trustees and executors; and so on.

However, the complex and difficult questions of a more personal nature can only be answered by wealth owners themselves. How much to pass on? How much to keep for retirement? When is a good time to give? How much to give to which children, to step-children, to philanthropic interests? Can children be trusted and empowered? Should they take over the family business? Should they be trustees? Can they decide what to do with what they receive or must limits and rules be imposed?

Advisors can provide many ways to save on taxes, or set up complicated legal structures. Reality is, however, that advisers are only there to implement the decisions. They should not and cannot make the decisions for the wealth owner.

Distribution: Equity and Fairness

Children often (maybe subconsciously) measure the love of their parents by how much they receive compared with their siblings. Does this mean that wealth can only be transferred to them in equal parts? No matter how equally parents try to deal with their children, the fact remains that some assets cannot be divided and that, long term, children will be unequal. Some will take more risk with their investments; some will have a frugal lifestyle; some will have special gifts and talents; and some will have more children than others.

Fairness is a better measurement when it comes to distribution. Fairness is not about how much or how little different people receive. It is about how decisions on wealth transmission are made. Fairness could be achieved by including the children in the decision; by respecting their choices and commitments; or by finding ways to help them live a happy life, quite apart from how much they inherit.

Passing on Legacy Assets

"Legacy assets" are items with a high emotional value attached to them. This emotional attachment can, for one or more individuals, outweigh the purely monetary value of the asset. Legacy assets can be a house, a family business, a painting, an estate, etc. Typically they have been in the family for one or more generations and are cherished by family members. They are part of both the family's history and its identity.

There are three particularly delicate aspects to consider when dealing with the transmission of a legacy asset. First, decide whom to leave it to. Will it go to just one of the descendants or to all of them collectively? One person may not have the competence needed to nurture it; but with more co-owners, more conflicts may arise.

Second, provide sufficient income for the recipient(s) to be in a position to take care of the asset. Many heirs receive fabulous properties but no money to maintain them. Finally, a way should be found to compensate the others fairly when only one receives both the legacy asset and the money to maintain it.

Letters of Wishes, Donor's Intent, Ethical Wills

In 1986, Warren Buffett said: "A very rich person should leave his kids enough to do anything but not enough to do nothing." His meaning was clear: not all of his wealth will be transferred to his children. Though not all parents have the same philosophy, what's particularly important is to transmit the family values that accompany the wealth.

A written explanation of these values can constitute a powerful ethical guide for succeeding generations. Imagine this situation: When Maria turned 19, her grandfather passed away. She felt empty and bereft. But a few days later, when his will was read, she learned that she had inherited some shares in the family business. With them came a letter from her grandfather: "My dear Maria, here are some shares in the business your grandmother and I started long ago. It was small then, but thanks to our family's work and strong ownership commitment, it has grown over the years. It is my wish and my hope that it remains a prosperous family business for many generations to come. It is now your turn to treasure it. I trust you. With all my love, Granddad." Maria knew she would never sell the shares. Her own children now look after the business.

Communication

While people of wealth have the option of communicating their testament before their passing, in reality this is not often done. There are many reasons. The issues may be difficult to explain. They may fear for their relationship with those left out. They may want to keep control. Or they may simply want to avoid family fights in their twilight years.

It is difficult for parents to tell their children they will not be treated equally, and why. How do you tell the oldest son that his younger brother will take over the business? Many heirs receive this devastating news shortly after the death of their parent, already a difficult time. They have no explicit warning, no preparation, and now they know they will never receive an explanation.

No matter how difficult these conversations are they should take place. An open courageous discussion is a truly valuable gift. There may be tears or anger. But healing can happen while somebody who loves them is still around to help.

Conclusion

We can never fully master the conditions that surround our lives, as our control over the world is limited, temporary, and often illusory. Although our environment considerably influences our well being, it is the mind itself that translates circumstances into happiness or suffering. In fact, one's state of mind can actually override outer circumstances. We can be deeply unhappy even though we "have it all" and, conversely, we can remain strong and serene in the face of hardship.

We must however be aware that a "selfish-happiness" can never lead to genuine well-being as it is a contradiction in terms. Selfishness is one of the root causes of suffering.

Being altruistic leads to a "win-win" situation. Loving, kindness and compassion are the most positive and fulfilling of all emotions. These emotions also help others as they inspire us to act in ways beneficial to those around us. Studies conducted on hundreds of subjects have revealed that there is an undeniable correlation between selflessness and happiness.[1] People who are the most altruistic also appear to be the happiest.

Conclusion

Obviously, our wealth, power, and skills impact the effect that our selfishness or altruism can have on our family and on the world. Those of us who have influential means need to be all the more.

How can we create a more compassionate family and society? This process begins with oneself. People who are at peace with themselves will naturally establish a greater harmony within their family, their work place, their neighborhood, and, circumstances permitting, society at large.

We need to transform ourselves to better transform the world.

Matthieu Ricard

---

1. Diener, E. and Seligman, M.E.P. Very Happy People. *Psychological Science*, 2002, 13: 81-84

ADDITIONAL READING

Family Business: Key Issues, Denise Kenyon-Rouvinez and John L. Ward, Palgrave Macmillan, New York, NY, USA, 2005

The World We Want: New Dimensions in Philanthropy and Social Change, Peter Karoff, AltaMira Press, Landham, MD, USA, 2007

Wealth, Stuart E. Lucas, Wharton Publishing, Upper Saddle River, NJ, USA 2006

Sharing Wisdom, Building Values: Letters from Family Business Owners to Their Successors, Denise Kenyon-Rouvinez, Gordon Adler, Guido Corbetta and Gianfilippo Cuneo, Family Enterprise Publishers, Marietta, GA, USA, 2002

The Monk and the Philosopher: A Father and Son Discuss the Meaning of Life, Jean-Francois Revel, Matthieu Ricard, John Canti and Jack Miles, Schocken Books, New York, NY, 2000

The Richest Man in Babylon, George S. Clason, Penguin Putnam, New York, NY USA, 1926

Rich Dad, Poor Dad, Robert T. Kiyosaki, Warner, New York, NY USA, 1997

The Gospel of Wealth, Andrew Carnegie, Applewood Books, Bedford, MA USA, 1998 (originally 1889)

The Way to Wealth, Benjamin Franklin, Applewood Books, Bedford, MA USA, 1986 (originally 1758)

THE AUTHORS

Swiss-American expert in the field of family business, **Denise Kenyon-Rouvinez** is a senior associate of the Family Business Consulting Group, Inc.® (FBCG). She is co-author of *Who, Me?* (Family Enterprise Publishers), *Family Business – Key Issues, 2005* (Palgrave Macmillan) as well as the project leader and principal author of *Sharing Wisdom, Building Values – Letters From Family Business Owners To Their Successors, 2002* (Family Enterprise Publishers). In recent years she has also published articles on governance issues and on serial business families. www.efamilybusiness.com.

Matthieu Ricard has lived in the Himalayan region for the last thirty-five years. After completing his doctoral thesis in 1972, he decided to forsake his scientific career and concentrate on Tibetan Buddhist contemplative practice. Since then, he has lived in India, Bhutan and Nepal with the greatest living teachers of that tradition and became the disciple and attendant of Dilgo Khyentse Rinpoche (one of the most eminent Tibetan masters of our times). Matthieu is a Buddhist monk and, since 1989, he has acted as the French interpreter for His Holiness the Dalai Lama. He is the author of several best selling books including *Animal Migrations* (Hill and Wang, 1969), *The Monk and the Philosopher* (Schocken, 1999), *The Quantum and the Lotus* (Crown, 2002), *Happiness, A guide to Developing Life's Most Important Skill* (Little, Brown and Co, New York; Atlantic Press, London).

The Authors

John L. Ward is the co-founder and principal of the Family Business Consulting Group, Inc.® and clinical professor at Kellogg School of Management (Chicago, USA). He is the author of several leading texts on family business, *Keeping the Family Business Healthy, Creating Effective Boards for Private Enterprises, Strategic Planning for the Family Business, Perpetuating the Family Business, Unconventional Wisdom* and *Family Business: Key Issues* (with Denise Kenyon-Rouvinez.) He is also an author of a collection of booklets, *The Family Business Leadership Series*, each focusing on specific issues family businesses face. www.efamilybusiness.com.

Gabs is a cartoonist and the author of a number of books. His work appears in magazines, books, and a variety of business publications. His cheeky cartoons speak for themselves. www.gabs.fr

Thierry Lombard is from the sixth generation of a family business established in 1796 in Geneva (Lombard Odier Darier Hentsch & Cie, private bankers). He has a passion for family businesses, and has initiated five books on the subject. A member of the board of the FBN, Managing Partner of the bank since 1982, and Senior Partner since 1995, he sits on a number of boards of directors. He is also active in many humanitarian, medical, and environmental foundations.

INDEX

Advisors, 32, 50, 72, 82, 96, 100, 106
Allowances, 66
Aristotle, 18
Assets, 48, 50, 74, 90, 108, 110
Beliefs, 34, 36, 44
Benchmarking, 74
Capital, 36, 38, 52, 66, 98, 100
Charity, 62, 66
Chores, 66
Communication, 52, 72, 78, 102, 114
Conflict Management, 64
Cousins, 50, 52, 54, 56
Dalaï Lama, 16, 20
Denial, 98
Discussions, 26
Distribution, 108
Dividends, 66, 72
Education, 40, 50, 68, 78, 100, 102
Emotional health, 28
Empowerment, 40
Equity, 72, 105
Estate planning, 50

Ethical wills, 112
Ethics, 16, 18
Exit strategies, 76
Fairness, 64, 108
Family constitution, 38
Family foundation, 100
Family meetings, 66, 102
Family office, 100
Financial Literacy, 66, 102
Gifts, 34, 48, 64, 108
Grandchildren, 50, 96
Greed, 16
Heirs, 72, 110, 114
Heritage, 36, 54, 66, 102
Identity, 24, 68 86 110
Information, 64, 82
Inheritance, 52, 80, 86, 92, 102
In-laws, 32, 50, 96
Kilpatrick, Andrew, 72
Layard, Richard, 18
Legacy, 92, 110
Letters, 66, 68, 112
Lifestyles, 46, 62, 76, 108
London School of Economics, 18
Managing money, 24

Motivation, 16, 88, 90
Nepotism, 54
Next generation, 40, 48, 52, 56, 66, 90, 98
New money, 28
Philanthropy, 62, 66, 102
Physical security, 28, 68
Portfolio, 74
Responsibilities, 12, 24, 30, 72, 80, 100
Retirement, 76, 106
Siblings, 50, 52, 56, 108
Society, 20, 28, 32, 38, 88, 100, 118
Spiritual wealth, 36
Staff, 100
Step-children, 106
Stewardship, 68, 90
Successors, 30, 50, 54
Taxes, 50, 52, 106
Transmitting wealth, 106-114
Twain, Mark, 102
Vocation, 100
Wealth creators, 28, 34, 44, 56, 72
Work ethic, 28